The Ch

A Poetry Memoir

by

Carolina Hospital

Arte Público Press
Houston, Texas

This volume is made possible through grants from the City of Houston through The Cultural Arts Council of Houston, Harris County.

Recovering the past, creating the future

Arte Público Press
University of Houston
452 Cullen Performace Hall
Houston, Texas 77204-2004

Cover design by James F. Brisson
Cover art "La distancia del sonido / The Distance of the Sound, 1994"
by Ana Albertina Delgado

Hospital, Carolina, 1957–
    The Child of Exile: A Poetry Memoir / by Carolina Hospital
      p.   cm.
   ISBN 1-55885-411-8 (pbk. : alk. paper)
    1. Cuban Americans—Poetry. 2. Women immigrants—Poetry.
I. Title.
PS3608.O8C48 2004
811'.54—dc22
                                                    2004041087
                                                       CIP

∞ The paper used in this publication meets the requirements of the American National Standard for Information Sciences—Permanence of Paper for Printed Library Materials, ANSI Z39.48-1984.

4 5 6 7 8 9 0 1 2 3   10 9 8 7 6 5 4 3 2 1

For my beloved
Carlos, Nicole, Sonora

Contents

Acknowledgments

With many thanks to the magazines and anthologies in which the following poems originally appeared:

A Century of Cuban Writers in Florida: "The Gardener"
The Black Swan Review: "To James Wright"
The Caribbean Writer: "First Snows"
Confrontation: "An Unexpected Conversion"
Cuban American Writers: Los Atrevidos: "El Trópico," "Coquina"
El Puente: "Distance" (in Spanish translation)
Forkroads: "On the Death of Roberto Valero"
In Other Words: Literature by Latinas in the U.S.: "Hell's Kitchen," "On the Last Stretch of the Journey," "For a Sister Here"
Linden Lane Magazine: "Blake in the Tropics," "Modern Faith," "Sonora," "Waters," "Madonna," "Communion," "A Poem of Thanks," "Recipe for Love," "Tabebuias in Bloom," "Mango Madness" (Under title "July Mangoes")
Looking for Home: Women Writing About Exile: "Freedom"
Mid-American Review: "Near Pigeon Key," "Scattered Wings"
Orchard: "Geography Jazz"
Prairie Schooner: "The Lost Hammock," "A Daughter for Raisa," "How the Cubans Stole Miami"
Rio Grande Review: "Sorting Miami," "Whale Harbor Inn"
The Americas Review: "Dear Tía," "Finding Home," "Alma Mater," "The Old Order"
The Miami Herald: "Savannah Risotto"
Windhorse: "Sand Dollar Island"

Heartfelt thanks to Nicolás Kanellos and everyone at Arte Público Press for their support, and to all my colleagues at Miami Dade College, my friends, my sisters, my parents, and my daughters, for putting up with a million readings throughout the years. Special thanks to Belkis Cuza Malé for her inspiration and to Carlos E. Medina for his constant encouragement, perfect suggestions for revisions, and unconditional love.

Gestation

There is a man sprawled at the edge of the sea
But don't think that I'm going to describe him as a drowned man.
— Heberto Padilla

Hell's Kitchen

for Angel Cuadra and Reinaldo Arenas

The words drip down his lips:
Una Revolución sin odio.
A Revolution without hatred
is what he wanted.
In that dark cell, he learned to forgive.
For 15 years, Angel forgave his youth
as it abandoned him, piece by piece.
He gave away his intimacy.
Ernesto helped him to write metaphors of love
that fit into a matchbox.
The words flew on the wings of angels
and carried away his anger with his passions.
He stood firmly on the damp ground,
as Reinaldo scattered with the sand.
Reinaldo found no angels,
only humans addicted to desire,
looking for the sum of all delights
in a place where no delights are possible.
The untempered pleasures of the flesh
offered him respite,
but when I met him, death was already waiting.
He had left hell to enter its kitchen
and there he died,
still eager as a 12-year-old boy.
Perhaps, one day angels and kings will meet
and need not speak.

A Daughter for Raisa

(A Eulogy)

Raisa Teresa Santana was pronounced dead
today, in Miami.
I never met her, nor heard of her before,
yet her story unraveled mine.

To her, the island was no tropical jewel
but an insular piece of land
surrounded by waters with no outlets.
This moat that delighted tourists
left no strip of shore unguarded,
with a channel so wide, it swallowed
her screams with my restless dreams.
She had witnessed the powers of those waves,
but preferred their unpredictable passions
to the idleness of a slow, ponderous end.

I suppose that's what Raisa thought
on May 7, 1993, when she took to the sea on a raft.
She brought her son, Frank, and her boyfriend,
who soon plunged into the wet darkness
chasing hallucinations.
She held on to hers a while longer.

Earlier, she had written:
Sometimes, we just have to laugh at it all.
What are we going to do,
if not take it easy
and go on with the rhythm of life?

Those words were lost in a dry wind
and the daily encounter with
empty shelves and battered lives.
Dressing in armor to survive
drove her to the sea,
a sea she knew little about,
a sea she had never befriended,
or she would have known better
than to accept its salty milk.
She gave her son the last food and water
and wiped the sweat from his brow.
Her own frail body became dehydrated.
Her brain swelled from the yearning
but her armor had grown
too thick, too heavy to cuddle him.
She placed an arm over him instead,
fell unconscious on his lap.
For hours, he must have watched her,
fate taunting him
to be a pall bearer.

A cool spray anointed his skin.
A nine-year-old boy was spared.
The passing ship heard his mother's breath.
Raisa never awakened to see the other shore,
my shore.

Soon, she will be forgotten,
another statistic,
not of the sea, but of an island
guarded by fears and desires.

I sit comfortably now,
at the bow of my motorboat.
I think of Raisa and the sea.
No crossing could separate her world from mine.
The same spirited wave that thrust her son on my shore,
will, one day, carry my daughters back to hers.

Brothers' Psalm

(On the shooting down of four
Brothers to the Rescue)

My heart is overwhelmed,
lead me to a rock higher than me,
a rock where I can see
the winged chariots falling,
followed by a thousand more.

I am weary of my crying:
my throat is dried:
mine eyes fail. . . .

Ignited with hatred, missiles
scattered the four brothers into the sea.
Parchments ablaze with scribbled yearnings
sent their smoke signal into the horizon.
Only a few received the message.

Deliver me out of the mire
and let me not sink.

Like spring blossoms
floating down over
paths of quiet desperation,
their words descended on peeling benches,
dusty curbs,
dilapidated rooftops.

Let those that accuse be put to shame.
Let those that rejoice in our pain
be confounded.

In our pews, crammed facing the altar,
we watch the young marine deliver the flag;
trumpets resound,
and the echo kicking within me
announces the beginning of death without.

In thee, Oh Lord, do I put my trust:
Let me never be put to confusion.

Only one of every four survives the crossing.
Without a white stone, the rest
become part of the straits,
waters that separate affliction from expectation.

The enemies,
violence covers them as a garment.
Their eyes stand out with fatness.
They set their mouths against the heavens.
The ungodly prosper in their world.

In our world,
the rock sits high,
it lets us see beyond the fires,
beyond the edge of darkness.

Freedom

for Belkis Cuza Malé

For 20 years they hid your words
afraid of you,
a young girl from Guantánamo,
the daughter of a cement factory worker.

They silenced poems of
cinderellas and silver platters,
frightened by your beautiful people
and portraits of sad poets.

Now, far from your island and them,
your poems shout without restrictions.
But the words remain unheard.
Here, a poem
doesn't upset anyone.

Sorting Home

For twenty years I've stared my level best
To see if evening—any evening—would suggest
A patient etherized upon a table;
. . . I simply wasn't able . . .

—C. S. Lewis

Dear Tía

I do not write.
The years have frightened me away.
My life in a land so familiarly foreign,
a denial of your presence.
Your name is mine.
One black and white photograph of your youth,
all I hold on to.
One story of your past.

The pain comes not from nostalgia.
I do not miss your voice urging me in play,
your smiles,
or your pride when others called you my mother.
I cannot close my eyes and feel your soft skin;
listen to your laughter;
smell the sweetness of your bath.
I write because I cannot remember at all.

An Unexpected Conversion

Mother hid from us the blue and white beads
her nanny, Brigida,
had giver her, and the plate of
pennies in honey under the Virgin's skirt.
She rarely spoke about the island,
never taught us to cook black beans.

Father played Stravinsky and Debussy on Sundays.
Once, he relented and taught us the guaguancó.
He swore, as she did, they would never go back.
He's thirty years in exile and
about to retire.

But today, mother and I sit in the garden.
She rests on the edge of an old rusted swing
and speaks of reconstruction,
of roads and houses; "I know they'll
need an experienced engineer," she says looking at dad.
Her hair blows gently in the breeze.

I've never seen her look so young.
I've never felt so old.

Sorting Miami

I pale my cheek against the pane
as the runway jolt blurs us into our city.
—Ricardo Pau-Llosa

I watch them unnoticed
from the cement railing outside
the José Martí YMCA, its glass doors locked for the day.

Tomatoes, limes, onions
hang in cellophane bags
from the rusted van.

Crates of papayas and avocados
surround this old vendor still smiling
after 11 years on the same street corner.

Friends take turn in the shade
exchanging stories
from a distant canvas.

A middle-aged woman, fighting a lost battle,
protects herself
with her red umbrella.

A young woman struggles
to push the baby carriage
along the brick sidewalk.

A Jeep pulls up
to buy its share
of the tropics.

I understand their voices,
and the silhouette of the vendor
could easily be that of my uncle, dead in Havana.

But in minutes,
I drive across a deep fissure
in the asphalt.
I wonder, how long will I be able
to step into this mirror of a city
and return home in one piece?

Finding Home

I have traveled north again,
to these gray skies
and empty doorways.
Fall, and I recognize
the rusted leaves descending
near the silence of your home.
You, a part of this strange
American landscape with its
cold dry winds,
the honks of geese and
the hardwood floors. It's more
familiar now than
the fluorescent rainbow on the overpass,
or the clatter of políticos at the corner,
or the palm fronds falling by the highway.
I must travel again,
soon.

Distance

Distance has made of us all strangers.
Another cousin I've never met
phones mother again from Havana.
After a life of silence,
he is begging
to be flown out of the island
even on the wings of Icarus.
He calls mother *tía* and she
opens her heart, so carefully sealed
after years of homesick nights.
A temporary visa and fear in his pocket,
he wanders the streets of Quito,
searching for the painful familiarity
he left behind.
In Lima, he is greeted by friends.
He is no longer alone.
We are sure he will make it,
wait his turn to reach us.
No.
Carlos has gone home,
back to Havana,
to his wife and daughter
and the habitual echoes of empty rooms.

Geography Jazz

Yes! We abandon
the pastel façades,
the curves,
the sculptured towers
on the Beach.
Those glass doors
edged with flamingos
take us
Yes!
to another city
we recall
through
secondhand
memories.
Yes!

Mongo's hands,
ecstatic pain,
he beats the conga
we rise
we beat the tables
he rises
we sweat
he shouts
we shout
Yes!
he succumbs.
His skin is gray
taut
like the old hide
on his drum.

But now I hear
him
Yes! Pérez Prado.
She wants a mambo.
Who?
Lupita.
What's wrong with Lupita?
What does she want?
To dance.
They won't let her dance.
No?
But now she can dance,
here she is dancing.
Yes, yes, yes!
She wants that mambo.
1 2 3 4 5 6 7 8
arms to the sky,
she wants a mambo, a delicious mambo.

A mambo in sax?
It's Chocolate,
a thief in the dark,
playing between chords,
stealing melodies.
Chocolate and synthesis,
syncreticism,
sin,
sin of the Caribbean, no
limits, no regrets.
One escalating fusion
as sweet as chocolate.

Yes!
I hear them.
Mongo
Dámaso
Chocolate
I hear them all.
It's a bright place
and water sets no boundaries,
and time poses no obstacles.

The Child of Exile

Only weeks ago he finally stopped
looking for the shadows of Havana
palm fronds outside his door.
But now, for the first time in
thirty years, he speculates
about a home that isn't his.
By night, he dreams of fogless mirrors
and migratory birds.
He writes poems about forgotten relatives,
tobacco pickers and sugar cane fields.
He has packed his bags with resurrected
images of tiled houses,
white dunes and baroque cathedrals.

Waters

I too am now haunted by waters

clear waters
over a smooth stone or a root,
a warm pool still in the sand,
waves grazing the driftwood,
low tide,
waters ebbing and high tide flowing,
rain,
a busy brook,
breaking waters,
a stormy lake,
a gushing waterfall,
snow waters,
icicles off the rocky hillside,
a long cool drink in August,
more rain,
droplets on the asphalt,
a warm shower at midnight,
a downpour

and rafters drifting at sea.

The Old Order

A man enters through the kitchen
and slams the door behind him,
as if afraid of letting the outside in.

Onions and peppers simmer,
fries and plantains sizzle,
pork grease drips off the window panes.

He places the yellowed cap on the Formica
and waits his turn.
Finally, he hollers above the clatter;
a young plump waitress serves him a mountain of rice.

After his meal, he wipes the grease off his lips,
gulps down his expresso and
shouts his good-byes.
Outside now, he tilts his cap and walks away with ease.

First Snows

From his second floor apartment
with its cathedral ceilings,
an herb garden,
and dusty first editions,
she steps out into
a Christmas card
with its snow covered walkway
leading to a yellow shingled house
and a red mailbox, empty.
He guides her to an open field
to find the white ground has covered
the tracks of laughing school children.
Instead they watch the flurries play
and follow the railroad tracks.
Dense with thought,
as if jelled by the cold,
they return home.
At dusk, she stares out
at the white silence of his town.
She turns to him
but she is frightened by the vision:
a reflection on the pane.
She looks away and dreams,
south.

The Hyphenated Man

Do you wake up each day
with an urge for a bagel
with café con leche?
Do you flip back and forth
through *The Miami Herald* comparing every word
to *El Nuevo Herald*?
Do you circle around back alleys
trying to decide between McDonalds and
Pollo Tropical?
Do you feel guilty buying Cuban bread
at Publix,
while getting a cheesecake at Sedanos?
At Thanksgiving, do you creep into the kitchen
to put mojito on the turkey,
and then complain at Christmas because
there's lechón instead of turkey?
Do you find yourself Two-Stepping
to salsa beat and dancing guaracha
to every other jazz beat?
Does your heart skip a beat for Sonia Braga
while longing wistfully for the days of Doris Day?
If so my friend,
then you are the hyphenated man.
Yes, H-Y-P-H-E-N.
The hyphenated man
lurks beneath that confident exterior,
and it's time you consider
Hyphens Anonymous,
where the confused straddlers find refuge
and solace.
They meet once a week,
talk Spanglish to their hearts' content,
eat mariquitas with hot dogs, and

cuban coffee with Dunkin Donuts,
without explanations or alienations.
Not the twelve step program,
but the three step dilemma.
Join today and
get off the see-saw,
jump off the fence,
slide down the hill,
cross the bridge,
get into the circle,
turn from the mirror.
Don't get off the wagon,
get on the hyphen.
Do not delay.
Hyphens Anonymous can help you forget
who you are
or better
who you wish you could be.

The Gardener

I sit on the crisp grass
and slowly pull the weeds
around the newly planted
Manila palms and purple heather.
The dirt sneaks
into the creases of my skin.
A gray covers the skies.
I let the scent of the warm soil,
the humidity in the air,
the stillness before the summer shower
transport me north
to the mountain forest,
of rhodedendrums and spruce pine,
south to la finca,
with its cafetales and sugar cane fields.
For an instant, I exist in three spaces.
Back in my garden, I look around.
I realize it doesn't matter.
The hibiscus and bouganvilleas
I have planted
are blooming.
In any soil,
they are the same,
as long as they grow
unfettered.

Tía Mía

I write because I cannot remember at all.

That is the last line of the first poem,
the first poem I ever wrote,
the first letter I never sent.

That was 15 years ago.

Tía has come to visit.
We have finally met.

Her hair is white yet silken,
held away from her eyes
by two tiny butterfly pins.

I'm not sure what I expected.
A harsher look, an angrier stare perhaps.

Her eyes, crystalline blue,
are deep and deceiving,
like the cool calm lake
I swam in, pregnant,
on those hot hazy months of summer.

She likes to tell stories,
forty years of stories,
of endless days caring for our ailing grandmother,
of cans of cheap paint and daily lines at the bakery,
of buckets of water hauled from the street below,
and of how they forbid her to speak,
nor to think about the children,
the children
she used to prime in her schoolroom.

Tía has returned to the island.
I can hardly recall
the lilt in her voice.

I never expected I would want
to seal my heart.

How the Cubans Stole Miami

The Cubans have stolen Miami.
("Will the last one to leave
bring the American flag?")
And from whom did we steal it?

From the Basque sailor who
gave Biscayne its name?
Or perhaps from the Spanish missionaries who lived
with the mosquitoes by the swampy bay?

In all fairness, we must admit
we stole it from the Tequesta or the Seminoles,
natives, driven north by
Andrew Jackson or south into the sea.

No, perhaps we stole it from the Spaniards
sent back to Havana after 300 years
of calling Florida home.
(And we complain about still being
in exile after only forty-four.)

If we didn't steal it from the Indians or the Spaniards
it must have been the Conks,
Bahamians who built the railroads with hands of coal
while being told to be more Negro like their neighbors
to the north.

I know, we stole it from
Flagler, Tuttle, Merrick and Fisher
who catered to the rich but never to the Jewish.
(Only in Miami is a Jew an Anglo.)
If I see one more photo of Domino Park
I'll turn into a Jew.

Was it he, papi, who stole Miami?
He, who engineered from the Bacardi building to
One Biscayne Tower
and every school addition from Edison
to Homestead High?

No, it must have been my mother.
(What was it Joan Didion wrote,
"a mango with jewels?"
Poor mother, so lean and trim.)
She spent 34 years volunteering
(Sacándole el kilo, my father would sneer.)

The Museum of Science,
Viscaya,
The Youth Center,
The Archdiocese,
Ballet Concerto,
La Liga Contra el Cáncer,
The Mailman Center.
(A tour of Miami, you ask?)

Enough! says my dad,
locking up his checkbook tight.
"We're retiring out of Miami."
A new phenomena,
"Cuban Flight,"
not to be confused with "White Flight."

If the Cubans have stolen Miami
and it's time they paid their dues,
then . . .

If I see one more photograph of Domino Park
who knows what I might do.

Sitting Still

I abandoned and forgot myself,
Laying my face on my Beloved.
                              —John of the Cross

The Lost Hammock
after Diego Vicente Tejera

On a dusty curb in Alacranes,
she sat with the childhood friend
who understood her silent dreams.

Twenty years, two islands and a husband
between them, she is drowning alone
in the middle of a tropical scream.

She is only to blame for not believing
that life comes
in grand gestures and passionate desires,

that kindness is foolish
and humble acceptance
a crime.

Her husband, he stumbles about her.
Una vida con miedo es una vida a medias.
A fearful life is a life half-lived.

Hummingbirds flitter among the trumpet vines
and the oak branches offer
their shade to this man, wandering still.

He can't recognize their gentle gestures
nor hear the silent brook
flowing without his consent.

In his search for an oasis
full of emeralds and rubies,
he has failed to notice

the sweet taste of sugar cane on her lips
and the strength of dawn
in her hazel eyes.
She waits,
lost in the memory
of that dusty road in Alacranes

where home meant a
porch nearby and
the scent of gardenias under her bedroom window.

Mornings

The useless dawn finds me
in a deserted street corner.

—Jorge Luis Borges

Dusk has settled on too many nights
when you have watched me expose our hungry hearts.
You have listened to poor excuses,
and trembled in your sleep, afraid of defeat.

I cannot say I have found the clarity
that comes to you at daybreak,
but I have seen its face:
a crystal vase with a spray of lavender orchids,

a breeze through the windowpane,
the cool surface of this marble table
where I write. I caress it.

I watch before me, colors
that burst into trees,
and I learn to wait.

El Trópico

for H. and A.

The amateur riders exchange glances
from the Trojan horses
that have led them here.
They look down
at their lost destiny
to where the palms drift in the salty breeze
while the children run barefoot
at the river's edge
or hide in the hammock
pretending to be captains of some grand galleon.
Their legs surround
the ample strength of these horses
that pull them closer to the forest,
wanting to get lost among the branches.
But afraid of being betrayed once more
the riders take control of the reins.

Southern Mood

The young man from New Jersey,
his eyes, dark wells of pride,
his smile, a cascade of delights,
speaks of his mother's southern cooking.
From Paris, London, and New York,
he has come full circle,
South,
to find a taste of Africa.
He is a chef of culinary evolution,
a master blender of cultures,
an adventurer of the palate.
For us, he chooses lamb,
common in most African dishes.
At our table, we wait.
Wood, stone and canvas converge;
an echo of a slave ship?
Planks, ballast, sails across the seas,
carrying, carrying . . .

Before the chef sears the lamb chops,
he marinates them in honey and mustard.
Then, he caresses each side
with ancient Moroccan couscous.
The heat seals the history,
blood blending with honey,
Africa making itself at home
in Savannah, Miami, New Orleans.
The king and queen of Mardi Gras,
rest on a royal float of mashed parsnip.
Their entourage displays its bright finery:
bits of green and red peppers, corn,
okra, and yellow squash
form a circle of dizzying glitter.
Tonight, the lamb chops unmask,
lingering, lingering . . .

Whale Harbor Inn at Dusk

He leaned on the wooden railing
ignoring the fishermen below
cleaning their catch.
The girls scurried around him
to see the next boat approach the dock.
He had tried to comfort me
over cold shrimp
and couldn't disguise
a heaviness in his spirit.
He told me
life felt like an old jacket
that no longer fit.
I wanted to stand by him now,
but the crisp breeze off the sea
made me tired.
I sat at my bench,
resting my head on the railing
and watched him try to fly.

For a Sister Here

Six years ago I discovered her
in the ruins of the city,
wandering among the ashes
of burnt souls.
Then, I denied my sister,
a stranger.
I listened,
heard the silence of fear,
the sounds of aimlessness.
I could only wait,
wait for her to break the night.
One night, any night,
she called me.
"I'm worthless," she said.
What new words could I unleash
to keep her on the line.
I knew what she wanted.

911 found her,
babbling,
contorted in spasms by the phone booth.
In the ambulance, she was on her way out.
The I.V. lines replaced the coke lines,
the steel railings stiffened the whitish limbs,
powder-free air tubed up her nose.
My sister, confined
within the sterile order of life support
arrived.
At the hospital, I waited.
All night, many nights.
She could not remember her bruises,
her missing chain of the Sacred Heart,
her last meal five days earlier.

Finally, she came out
packed with weary promises.

It's four days before Christmas;
her daughter, a fly on her arm, sits
by the door, ready
for their two-week visit.
She never arrives.
It's easier to live
in the night,
where the dark conceals the ruins
and hides the residues of destiny.
Meaning splits in half and
the nearness of death
destroys all shame.
No longer my sister,
she becomes an accomplice
with the illusions,
falsehoods littered
across the cool counter of the bar.
Outside she tries to call home,
but she can't recognize the sidewalk.
Seven days and no word of her.
Will she get away this time?
Or will I find my sister
a hanging effigy
smiling upon the ruins?

On the Last Stretch of the Journey

You recovered the forgotten
smell of woman.

—Tania Díaz Castro

On the last stretch of the journey,
I held the reins so tightly
my palms ached
and the mare gasped for air.
She struggled until I relaxed.
At first, she raced madly
across the grazing fields.
Gradually, she settled
on a steady trot
that returned us to the stables.
Her freedom delivered mine.

"This is a moment of grace," said Father.
He held my hands and smiled,
as if my return after 18 years
was a gift I had delivered him.
A spoiled child had abandoned
the stained-glass windows
or sat waiting in an empty pew.
Now, he saw a woman approach him.
"Forgive yourself," insisted Father.
His hands on my head
released the fear.
I stopped fighting my will.

I embraced the void,
the one that follows me like a lost child.
I awakened from a scream
to find you searching for my purity.
You smelled my hair,

my naked flesh,
trying to uncover a memory.
I tumbled into your arms.
We made love.
You were surprised
by the child in my eyes.

The Age of Lovers

You married a child;
a child you married.

—Ruth Stone

I have always answered
you with silence,
afraid of losing
my own shadow.

Today, we have driven to the sea
in the early mist of an October day.
We read across the marble table,
transported to the city
of late bars and wars.
I, your Castor.
You, my philosopher and lover.

Only the breezes speak;
only our knees touch.
But in the silence of this morning,
I have finally found the words.

Glimpses

1

A breeze through
the cypress trees,
her breast pulses
to the flap of sails.

2

The moon grows large
after dusk.
He drops rose petals
on her bare back.

3

Rays of sun on each strand,
her hair hangs over his chest.
Their hearts are tangled
forever.

Recipe for Love

for Belkis and Heberto

After 25 years of marriage,
I thought I could offer
a recipe for love.

Tío has come to visit from Havana.
He tells me of his 43-year marriage
to the woman he met at a guest house,
after he was engaged to another,
the woman with whom he toasted
forty anniversaries
of hardships and betrayals,
the woman with whom he has met God.

We walk along the gravel path
leading to the jetties,
and I listen.

Still Married

Minutes before the alarm rings,
before I raise my heavy limbs
to measure out my day
in milk bottles and rice cups,
your warm thighs spoon against mine.

Across coffee mugs, bagels, and teenage angst,
you glance at me.
Your eyes speak of desire.

I struggle with pampers and a pair
of kicking legs, when you tug
at my belt buckle, pull me toward you,
and steal a kiss.

With an apron and hands smelling of onion,
you twirl me around the leather couch,
the guaguancó, like a puppeteer,
commanding our weary feet.

It's a spent day;
I am ready to lie still,
but you stir me:
a passionate embrace over a field
of rose petal sheets.

Running Water

As I slide her plump rolls
into the running water,
I ignore the clamor of my own aching body,
cantankerous after a long day's work.
You join me.
We gladly struggle
to clean behind her ears,
between the folds of flesh.
Her torso wriggles and writhes
with dripping pleasure.
Your hand touches mine.
We hold each other's eyes.
Beyond the moisture,
we kiss,
our lips slowly blossoming.

Twenty Springs

I

Twenty springs ago,
we embraced
under a bright rain.
We danced
among the seagulls.

Now, the winds are still.

My hair is too long.
I leave it, so you can dishevel it.

My laugh is too loud.
I unbind it, so you can anticipate it.

My tears are too delicate.
I gather them, so you can remove their trace.

My hands are too fragile.
I search for yours.

We walk together into the night.

II

After twenty years, I have
discovered what you knew all along,
that love is what brings us
to the edge of the sea,
that it is hard
to turn oneself inside out
only to find you recognize your lover
better than yourself.

But through the stumbling discoveries,
I know now that love,
real love,
is sitting still.

Communion

Women don't make History,
but at nine months they push it out of their bellies
then sleep for twenty-four hours
like a soldier on leave from the front.
                                        —Belkis Cuza Malé

Alma Mater

At half past three at school,
in an oversized blue T-shirt
and navy polyester shorts,
Nicole sees a crowd of mothers.

I see me,
six again with tears,
searching, my mother with a
flowery wide skirt and flats,
waiting in a '67 Ford,
under the same black olive trees.

I return to her
now
running, smiling, waving.
For hers are not hollow hallways.

They hold the echoes.

Coquina

Each Wednesday night, alone
we bathe in unison.
Again you ask
why our bodies do not look as one.

Your nipples, drops of flesh
that tomorrow will flow
down a warm river giving life
to both man and child.

Your torso, bare proportions of my own
without the darkness
that reveals passage
into an unknown land.

Your blue eyes look at me
perplexed
as I silently lather your hair.

Sand Dollar Island

Like a flooded swamp,
the beach lies gray.
Horseshoe crabs crawl along the sand in pairs.
The pelicans claim their rotted posts by the mangroves.
The heat turns air into steam and
the low tide trails the stench of decay.

But Nicole skips along the shore,
shouting every time
she detects another sand dollar.
She leans to pick up each one with care,
strands of her wet hair cooling the reddened shoulders.
The moon begins its rise
and we return quietly, listening
to the crackle of shells under our weight.

Back inside, she lays out the sand dollars on a newspaper.
The gray flower-like markings
resemble a child's tracing,
and she is mesmerized.
I can't hear what she is saying to her father,
but I am sure they are sailors exploring deep waters
on a lulling night that offers them no dangers.

Suddenly, one of the sand dollars,
the smallest,
crumbles in her hand.
Her eyes search for mine.
I see them slowly fill
with drops of fear.

Captiva

In the summer sea, Nicole's salty flesh
is appetizing.
The Persian God did not remove
the 99.9% of love required
to stop me from wanting to consume her.
We frolic in the waves.
She rests her head on my breasts,
hugging me tightly,
as if fearing what it will be like
to grow up.
With her blond strands under
her olive green hat and
bottle top sunglasses,
she looks up at me, waiting.

Four osprey above us
split the air.
One perches itself on a dead tree snag
on the edge of the Australian pine forest.
It looks out to the sea.
In the yellowish hue of sunset,
its white breast glistens
against the dark green foliage behind it.
The other ospreys fly above, whistling loudly,
but this one remains still,
its talons gripping the snag.
It too waits.

I am surprised by bliss.

First

A caterpillar waiting to fly.
A shell waiting to crack.
A tadpole waiting to croak.
A seed waiting to sprout.
Milk waiting to boil.
A cork waiting to pop.
A volcano waiting to erupt.

An incubator
with an auto response button:
Yes, I'm not feeling well.
No, I'm not feeling better.
Yes, it was a surprise.
No, we didn't plan it.
Yes, I'm happy.
Of course, I'm happy.

Don't run.
Don't get excited.
Don't drive the jeep.
Don't drink coffee or alcohol.
Don't take aspirin or penicillin.
Don't eat tomatoes or chocolate.
Do sleep more.
Eat more.
Rest more.
Laugh more.
Be happy.
Check all of the above,
then watch as
he rubs your belly
like a Buddha
filled with a cheap mixed drink.
Your center is grounded.

All energy channels to the core.
Everything becomes periphery.
You are physicist and physician,
poet and pod.
Pick the best metaphor
and what do you get?
Pregnant and published.

Third Trimester

The words will have to wait again.
Until the seedling grows its branches and
the morning dove stretches its wings,
the words will lie still.
They cannot help me now to push out the pain,
pain of a century of unspoken disappointments,
       of barbed wires
       exposed ribcages
       deadening screams.
Like a ritual
each night
I let the water flow over my flesh.
It awakens each pore,
arouses my motherhood.
The century is almost over.
Perhaps, we will outlive the night.

Communion

No one understands
why some nights,
like tonight,
the moon glows colossal
flaunting its craters,
mastering the night sky,
like the host monsignor
holds high above his head
during the Eucharist.
As I watch the lunar eclipse
I recall the breaking of bread,
the tinkling of the bells,
the scent of incense.
All actions combined into one.
Taking the bread, he said
"This is my body given to you."
Now, I offer her my body,
food to nurture her,
gift of the spirit
consecrated in the flesh.
She rejects it,
and so I turn back
to the moon
and pray
for her to return to the source.

Sonora

after Li-Young Lee

I watch her sleep,
impatiently,
waiting for her limbs to twitch,
a sign of near awakening.
What dreams can she be fathoming
after these mere three months of life?
I dare not disturb her peace.
It is time for her rest,
and mine.
Yet I yearn for her to break into a smile,
a wave of love covering her face;
a taste of heaven.
I sit nearby and observe her
longer than I should;
the blank page waiting.
She is a tiny measure of perfection,
my tiny measure,
a minuscule shell I manage to hold on to
while the others slip from my grasp,
swept away by the breaking waves:
perhaps, a royal bonnet
carried ashore by trawlers from deep waters,
or a harry triton hidden under a rock,
or my favorite banded tulip,
common in the grassy bays.
She moves.
I tuck in her blanket a little tighter.
God must be lonely now.
I am pleased.

Ritual

for Nicole

I pour the lime juice into the glass
bowl filled with chunks of cold grouper
and tiny pieces of cilantro, peppers, and scallions.
We will eat the ceviche tomorrow
over thin crackers, the juice
marinating our lips.

We will sit,
mother, father, daughter, sister,
around the wooden table,
a perfect square,
savoring each bite, each word,
each setting sun.

Soon Nicole's chair will be empty.

Not yet.
For a few more months, I will squeeze
the scent out of each lime.

Madonna

1

As you lay on the raw ground,
expelling your son,
did your body writhe like mine,
contorted by a metaphor?

When you nursed him from your sore breasts,
did you know then
you would witness his death,
bleeding on the cross,
a common criminal?

Tell me, Mary of Nazareth,
not even God could spare you,
the necessary agonies of life
and love?

2

I search for you in every portrait . . .
but you are always sad, melancholy.
(Some call it holy.)

On my canvas of words,
you would raise your child,
head back,
arms high in the air,
laughing with glee
at seeing God's kingdom
here on Earth.

If I could hold a paint brush,
I would color you tender,
kissing his flesh,
frolicking,
your garments flowing as you roam
in a field of miniature white roses.

3

I hear you scold him,
as you scolded us in Fátima and Medjugorje.
You yell out his name,
but he doesn't answer.

God has lent us all our children.

Monarchs in Flight

Once far over the breakers,
I caught a glimpse of a white bird
And fell in love
With this dream which obsesses me.

—Yosano Akiko

Near Pigeon Key

(where pigeons migrate to Florida from Cuba each spring.)

Seventy-year-old Cuban Royal Palms
share the coastline
with cabbage palms and slash pines.
Dead now from a freeze,
some stand bald
without their majestic feathers.
As I stare up at them,
I see ducklings pile out
of the holes and drop
thirty feet onto a tapestry of grass and needles.
The hollow stumps have become their homes
and I am filled with an unexplainable relief.

Blake in the Tropics

We leave the Jaragua hotel
in our stocking feet and shaven faces
to stumble over these bodies
yet to reach puberty.

They have turned dust into blankets
and newspapers into pillows
on a street edged in refuse.
Warm waves break against the sea wall,

never touching their bodies.
We are not in Blake's London and
the black on these boys
will not wash off with the dawn.

To James Wright

I cannot write of spring images,
late winters,
an old farmer,
a lake in Minnesota.

I only see empty porches
framed in concrete.

Scattered Wings

The bamboo blinds were swayed
only by the autumn winds.
— Princess Nukada (7th Century)

Dawn wakes me with a start.
The children lie still
behind the thick pine doors.
The moist night shirt
clings to the flesh beneath my breasts.
I creep out of the farm house
and rush down the rock path to the brook.
Sitting on the cold bank,
I splash water on my face,
down my neck,
over my arms and thighs.
I lick the sweet wetness
blending with the salt on my lips.
Nearby, a hummingbird flitters
among the hibiscus
unaware of my presence
or its desire.

Summer in the Nantahala Forest

I

Rhododendrons in bloom
follow the river's edge.
We row into the mist
only to watch it disappear.

II

A cloudy haze over the mountaintops
embraces the solitude.
The queen anne's lace clothing the roadside
fills us with expectancy.

III

Humid nights on cold white sheets,
our love grows
with the darkness.

IV

After a strenuous hike uphill
we reach the ridge.
We are greeted by sunlight and
a trail of miniature wild orchids.

V

On top of the large rock,
overlooking the hill,
you disrobe and hold
only your walking stick.
I watch you with delight.

VI

The trunk of the poplar tree, wide
and erect, makes its way up to the sun.
Its base rests by a river rock,
smooth and steady.

VII

The horse trail narrows.
If I try hard,
I can make out the foot trail
among the branches.

VIII

Waiting for the horses,
I hear a rooster crow.
I am visited by memories
of more cloudy days.

IX

The cicada cry out
day and night.
At dusk, the fireflies
tease us with their glow.

X

I look at her sit on the river stone.
She watches the cold stream
cascade over her legs.
We are both satisfied.

XI

In the midday heat,
he lays on the hammock
under the hemlock trees.
She quietly whittles next to him
unafraid of the bliss.

XII

The wooden cabin sits at the edge of the forest.
I sit on the porch memorizing
the hillside.
I will bring it back in dreams.

A Spring Baptism

Stepping over the path,
a rippling wave of fallen lavender blossoms,
I pass the jacaranda,
startled by the flight of blue jays
startled by my own presence.
It is almost dusk,
I must hurry.
The sun's rays, low,
crown my favorite royal poinciana.
The tree's tangled branches spread out
over the neighborhood
ablaze in dazzling hues
of orange and crimson against the background of
a few remaining verdant leaves.
For a few minutes
I stand motionless
as the leaves float around me like brocade.
I am filled with color.

Monarchs in Flight

Their small lightweight bodies
and large marbled wings
form a cloud of rusted gliders in the sky.
It is autumn.
They have assembled at night
to fly to a warmer winter.
They are the fifth generation,
destined to return to that chosen tree
of their forebearers.
Without memories of branches,
they dart South.
I await their visit each year.
I imagine their arrival
at that unfamiliar blossom
where they will settle if only a while.
If I disturb their rest,
a thousand silken wings
flitter around me.
But the news on the radio is alarming this year.
Many will not travel far this fall.
They will flutter aimlessly,
unable to land on the milkweed edging the road.
We have trampled on their
only refuge along the way.

Savannah Risotto

Like a courtly gentleman,
the risotto teases me
with its creamy blend of
rice and sunflower seeds,
smoothly spiced with challots
and sundried tomatoes.
With almost a side glance,
the risotto hints at nutmeg and curry.
Elevated "Low Country" cooking,
the chef called it,
"Southern Exposure."
I am truly hungry but I think,
not too much,
not too quickly, lest
I not be considered refined.
Then, I turn to the gritty cornbread
and buiscuits on the table.
They remind me of the scrappy
school girl who stepped into our truck
each morning smelling of homemade buiscuits
smeared in bacon grease.
This is home, I think again,
and the coy risotto slyly
reveals the possibilities.
I dive into pleasure.

Papaya Leaves

I don't know how long
the papaya plants will rest
against our kitchen window.
These hollow reeds have grown so tall,
they reach the second floor before
they burst open with bulbs of fruit.
Like giant starfish,
the leaves spread open
and sway.
I like to watch them when it rains.
The droplets dangle off their points.
The plants stretch high and wide and
on sunny days,
shade everything, including
my window pane.
I used to resent these large bright leaves
blocking my view.
But I've grown accustomed
to their face.

Mango Madness

Pickups pull up along the road,
beds full of mangoes.
Across the street, Jorge's mango trees entice me,
branches heavy with promise.
Dozens of mangoes on my kitchen counter,
so many, the house fills with a ripened odor.
I love to peel one after another
until my nails turn orange.
The pulp squeezes through my fingers
as I slice its thickness.
Before I toss out the seed,
I close my eyes and
suck at the remaining flesh.
The juices drip down my chin,
so sweet.

Tabebuias in Bloom

for José

Today is different.

When I pull around the corner
to approach Sonora's school,
I can't help but notice
the trees lined along the road.

They have burst into bloom,
all of them,
as if a curtain of rain had unveiled
an orchestra of trumpets.

I park beneath their branches,
like I do each morning.

Blasts of yellow
blare against the blue
as if God himself were coming.

They will not last the month, I think.

Sonora slows down
and traces each bell shaped flower
falling to the ground.
She reaches down for one
and deliberately mouths each syllable
Ta-be-bu-ia
gleaming with anticipation.

Clinging

In the secret of night
my prayer climbs like the liana,
gropes like a blind man,
sees more than the owl.

—Gabriela Mistral

Modern Faith

The yellow fog that rubs
its back upon the window panes.

—T.S. Eliot

It was easy at nine to believe
in burlap banners,
offertory prayers for world peace,
hymns out of tune.
But panes of stained glass
now filter the sunlight and
the human-sized crucifix
no longer hangs on the altar.
Fifteen years later,
she sits among the empty pews,
waiting.

On the Death of Roberto Valero

When I saw Francis wander the narrow streets
and dark alleys of Assisi, the other day,
I did not expect to find you,
barefoot like a beggar.

Then, I did not know of your questions
to this sacred mendicant,
nor that you would join him
in your wounds and your humility.

It's good to remember that we are divine,
you once said.

In your suffering,
you saw the face of Christ and
did not demand to be lowered from the cross.

When your body turned finite,
you did not pray for a cure,
but for a vision.
You did not pray to be spared,
but to be spared of radiation and resentment.

We dreamed
you were taken from us,
not by the plagues
and pestilences of medieval Assisi,
but by one of our own afflictions.

I searched for you,
Roberto, my Roberto,
who coined the name Carloslina
for Carlos and me,
husband and wife,

instead of brother and sister,
as you once thought,
who listened when we needed you to,
who publicly pleaded for reconciliation,
who comforted Reinaldo in *his* dying days.

You studied, wrote, married, bore children, and taught, all
before you were forty,
all in a foreign landscape of cold nights
and greetings in English.

No, Roberto,
you are neither defeat nor loss.
With your AIDS,
you too walked the streets of Jerusalem and Assisi.
Memories do not pass away easily,
and in your memories
you have given us another glance at God.

Epiphany
for Monsignor Jude O'Doherty

Like the Samaritan woman at the well,
I, too, did not recognize the face of God.
I doubted the meaning of stones
reassembled by human hands.

Six years, the bell strikes as
I cross the threshold toward an altar like water.

The lattice woodwork,
mangrove branches I bike under each Saturday,
forms a Gothic arch high above my head.
My arms are drawn up
to the stained-glass cross.

The sunlight spills
lavender and yellows across the granite floors,
spatters blues and greens on the stone walls,
emblazes the bronze evangelists;
a shifting canvas of mirrored skies and marbled seas.

Behind me, a thousand pipes and brass trumpets,
within immense mahogany wings, rise from the earth.

In this paragon of steel and stone,
the human and the divine cross;
the sacred grounds have been restored.

A Poem of Thanks

for Carlos

The ring awakens me.
Her voice so familiar calling me from sleep
becomes an aching chorus of angels
proclaiming I will be fine.

I do not tell her
that I have forgotten
how to use the future tense,
that what I want is to lie
still beneath the rains.

She calls me a survivor,
but I know I have not been to the front
nor languored in a dark basement
or a rancid cell.

Before the mirror, what remains
is an echo of an infant's lips suckling
from a body that was once whole.

I look away.
Darkness.
It cannot be put out.

He enters, quietly.
He lights a small candle beside me,
slowly combs the knots out of my tangled hands,
cleanses the scar across my broken breast.
My body grows limp like a dying child.

I bind myself to him.
I invoke his name.
I find my reflection restored in his eyes
and I understand.
Human love cannot be measured
but in the depth of God.

About the Author

Carolina Hospital is a Cuban American poet, essayist and fiction writer. She teaches writing and literature at Miami Dade College, where she was twice awarded Endowed Teaching Chairs. Her work has appeared in numerous national magazines and newspapers including *Prairie Schooner, Latina, The Washington Post,* and *The Miami Herald*. She has been published in more than a dozen anthologies including *Harper Collin's Hispanic-Americans, Florida in Poetry, Little Havana Blues,* and *In Other Words: Literature by Latinas in the U.S.* To date, she has published four books including: *Cuban American Writers: Los Atrevidos,* a ground-breaking anthology of Cuban Americans; *Everyone Will Have to Listen,* a bilingual edition of poetry by Tania Díaz Castro, translated by Hospital with Pablo Medina; and *A Century of Cuban Writers in Florida,* a seminal work for understanding the cultural history of Florida, edited with Jorge Cantera. She also participated with authors such as Carl Hiaasan, James Hall, Dave Barry and Edna Buchanan, in the *New York Times* Bestseller collaborative novel *Naked Came the Manatee.* Finally, she and her husband, Carlos Medina, co-authored their debut novel *A Little Love,* published by Warner Books, under the pen name of C. C. Medina.